The Novel Writer's Toolshed

for Short Story Writers

For Bob
With very best wishes
Happy Writing!
Della Galton
⤳x

About Della Galton

Della Galton is a novelist, short story writer and journalist. She's had over a thousand short stories published in the UK alone and she's run out of fingers to count her books on.

She is a popular speaker at writing conventions and the agony aunt for Writers' Forum Magazine.

When she is not writing she enjoys walking her dogs around the beautiful Dorset countryside and beaches.

Find out more about Della Galton, her books, speaking engagements & workshops, on her website, dellagalton.co.uk

The Novel Writer's Toolshed

for Short Story Writers

Your Quick-Read Guide To Writing Longer Fiction

Della Galton

soundhaven books

Published 2014, in Great Britain, by
soundhaven books
(soundhaven.com limited)

Text Copyright © Della Galton 2014

Please visit
www.soundhaven.com
for contact details

ISBN: 978-0-9568856-5-4

British Cataloguing Publication data:
A catalogue record of this book is available from
the British Library

This book is also available as an ebook.

For Gaynor Davies,
with grateful thanks for your help,
advice and friendship across the years.
love
Della

Contents

Introduction

The Short Story to Novel Toolshed was originally written as a series for Writers' Forum Magazine. It is aimed at short story writers who would like to write their first novel. It will also be useful for novelists who would like to write short stories. And it'll probably be useful to anyone who hasn't written much at all, but would like to try their hand at either short stories or novels. It is designed to show you the differences between the two forms.

This version has been amended and updated and includes brand new material. It is intended to be a quick guide for the writer who doesn't want to wade through a lengthy tome. It complements my more comprehensive guide, Moving On – From Short Story to Novel, published by Accent Press.

How The Toolshed Works

Every writer has certain tools at their disposal. We all in fact use the same tools when it comes to writing, but we're not necessarily that adept when we set out, particularly when making a transition from one type of writing to another. The tools may be the same, but their application is slightly different. This book is a little like an instruction manual, which I'm hoping might save you some time.

So, what exactly do we have in our toolshed? Well this particular toolshed is divided into shelves and on the shelves you will find the following tools:

- Shelf one: planning, plotting, pace and timescale
- Shelf two: setting; shelf three: characters and viewpoint
- Shelf four: dialogue
- Shelf five: the first page and beyond
- Shelf six: development, author voice and endings
- Shelf seven: structure and flashback
- Shelf eight: editing and revision
- Shelf nine: the title, the synopsis, the blurb
- Shelf ten: finding an agent or publisher.

If you like you can work through the entire toolshed, or you might prefer to go straight to the relevant shelf. But to begin let me take you on a whistle-stop tour of the toolshed. Let's examine some of the obvious differences between writing short stories and writing novels, as well as having a quick look at some of the available tools.

Short Stories Versus Novels What's the Difference?

Making the transition between writing short stories and writing your first novel isn't as simple as you might think. Or at least it wasn't for me. I'd had a fair amount of success with my short stories and I didn't think that writing a novel would present too much of a problem. Surely it was just a short story with more words, more characters and more plot, wasn't it?

No doubt, some of you are already sniggering at my naivety, and I was naïve. I made a lot of mistakes before I managed to write a publishable novel. Many of them were down to assumptions I had that simply weren't true.

Yes, there are similarities between the short story and the novel and yes many of the techniques used for one can be transferred successfully to the other, but there are an awful lot of differences too.

The object of this book is to help you avoid some of the mistakes I made. Let's take a quick look at some of the differences before we go into more detail about what's in the toolshed, and hopefully this will make your transition a little smoother than mine was!

Length

This is probably the most obvious difference. Not many short stories are longer than about 5,000 words and even a short novel is at least ten times longer than that. The average length for a novel – if there is such a thing – is somewhere between about 50,000 and 120,000 words, depending on the type of novel and the publisher's requirements.

Unlike a short story, which can be written and edited in a few days, a novel is going to take a substantial amount of time and work, which brings me on to my next point nicely.

Subject

What you write is always a fairly important question – time is our most precious commodity – but it's not quite as important when you're choosing what your next short story is about. After all, writing a short story takes significantly less time than writing a novel. We can afford to experiment a bit more. However, if you are going to spend a great deal of your precious time and energy on your novel – which you will if you're going to do it properly – then it isn't a bad idea to choose something you are passionate about. There are two main reasons for this:

1. If you are enjoying the writing, you are more likely to finish it.

2. If you don't end up selling it then at least you will
    have enjoyed its creation and hence won't feel
    your time would have been better spent doing
    cross stitch or playing golf!

I have no idea of the statistics on unfinished novels,
but I bet there are thousands of them, languishing in
desks or on computers across the country. They are
started in a flash of inspiration and then the author finds
they peter out at around 27,000 words, or perhaps worse,
are finished in 27,000 words.

The percentage of first novels that are published is
also very small. I have heard various figures quoted, but
I won't depress you with them. Besides, who really
knows? A great many writers don't even send their first
novels out to publishers and a great many more are told
by their publishers that although this is the eighth book
they've actually written, it will be marketed as their
debut novel.

This is not intended to put you off, far from it. Write
your novel, keep an eye on the market, but primarily do
it for the love of it.

My first novel, incidentally, which was written when I
was about twenty, is somewhere in our loft, along with
the other three novels I wrote before I managed to write
one that was publishable!

Right then, let's have a quick look at what's on each
of the shelves, whist keeping the differences between
short story and novel in mind.

Planning, plotting, pace and timescale

A short story plot, by its nature, needs to be kept fairly simple. There isn't enough room for it to be complicated. Generally a short story will tend to focus on a single event or theme.

If you are writing several thousand words you will need a much more developed plot, or perhaps one main plot and some interlinking subplots to sustain the length. Whereas a short story can follow a single idea, longer fiction tends to need more than one.

There isn't room to hang around too much in a novel either, but you do need to have a very good control of pace. Contrary to what I thought when I started my novel writing journey, there is no room for waffle. Every word must still count. For many short story writers, pace is the hardest thing to adjust to when they begin to write longer fiction.

Setting

Setting in a novel is much more important than it is in a short story. In certain types of novels, for example regional sagas, it is equally as important as character. I will cover setting in detail under Shelf Two. All I want to say here is that you need to show setting through the eyes of your viewpoint characters – do not paste it into your novel in blocks or your reader will probably skip it!

Characters and viewpoint

A short story of a thousand words almost certainly won't have more than two or three characters, one of whom will be the main character. There is a lot more room for characters in a novel although that doesn't mean you should attempt to have a cast of hundreds! You will still need to know whose story it is – this is perhaps even more important in a novel than a short story as it's much easier to lose focus – and *all* of your characters must be essential.

In a short story there is often only room for one viewpoint. In a novel there is room for more. Using the viewpoint of more than one character can add a great deal of depth to a novel if done with skill.

Dialogue

In a short story your reader will probably forgive you if your characters don't have recognisable and individual voices. In a novel, they probably won't. So character voice is one of the most important things to work on in longer fiction.

The first page and beyond

It's vital to get your first page right. It is just as vital not to get stuck on it. I have a personal theory that it's difficult to write the first page of your novel until you've written the rest of it. When I'm writing a short story I find the ending is the most difficult part. When I'm writing a novel I find it's the opposite. It's easy to write the last page, but very difficult to write the first.

Development, author voice and endings

Developing a story is fairly easy. The middle follows on naturally from the beginning – and so it is with novels, only it's much easier to end up with a saggy middle in a novel – this can be solved by careful control of pace and also, I think by strong author voice. Thankfully, while ending a short story is tricky, bringing a novel to a satisfactory conclusion is much easier.

Structure and flashback

How will you structure your novel? Deciding before you begin to write can help you to plan it. Structure is a short story writer's friend, but it's a novelist's *best* friend because there are far more options.

Your novel might have a prologue. It might be split into parts and it will probably have chapters. You're not limited to flashback. You can use flash forward too! It is great fun to play with time in a novel.

Editing and revision

The main difference between editing and revision of the two forms is time. A short story can be edited in a morning or an afternoon. A novel is much more unwieldy. Using a plan can help.

The Title, the synopsis, the blurb

A good title is always important, but it's more vital for a novel than a short story, as it's one of your key selling points. A great title can sell a novel. A bad one can cause it to sink without trace.

Most novelists I have spoken to hate writing a synopsis. This is something you rarely have to do for short stories but which is an essential part of a novelist's job. Or is it?

These days it's probably more important to be able to write a blurb. Has the synopsis taken over from the blurb? What's the difference? On Shelf Nine you'll find some examples of both.

Finding an Agent – Do you need one?

The short answer is no. You have never needed an agent for short stories and you don't necessarily need an agent for novels either, these days, but is it worth going alone? If you do want to look for an agent or a publisher, Shelf Ten, will show you how to proceed.

Shelf One

Planning, Plotting, Pace and Timescale

Once you've made the decision to write a novel the temptation is to sit down and begin writing immediately. But you will probably save yourself a lot of time and heartache if you do some preparation work first.

The amount you choose to do will vary depending on what type of writer you are. Some writers like to let the story develop and grow from the characters and setting and some prefer to have a detailed synopsis or outline to work from. You'll probably know which suits you best. But even if you don't work to a detailed synopsis, there are some questions you might like to ask yourself:

Do you have a big enough idea?

This is especially relevant if you've been used to writing short stories. But what exactly does this mean? Well to me it means having an idea that has a fair bit of depth. I don't want to start writing and then run out of things to say at 30,000 words. I'll choose a subject that interests me – so I'll be happy to do the research. Or I'll choose a subject of which I already have some personal experience.

My first published novel, Passing Shadows, was set against the backdrop of an animal sanctuary in Wiltshire. I had helped out at an animal sanctuary in Wiltshire so I was familiar with how they are run and I am passionate about animal rescue.

The novel wasn't about animal rescue, it was an emotional story about a girl who falls in love with the father of her best friend's child – only he doesn't know he's the father.

I don't have any experience of that scenario, I'm happy to say, but I did think I'd have enough conflict and emotion to sustain a novel length story.

Short story ideas versus novel ideas

Short story ideas are relatively simple. They often focus on one aspect of a character's life or on a specific problem they have. In a novel the stakes must be higher and the problem must be something that really matters and this takes more than five minutes to solve.

Test your idea

Try a mind map. Write down the basic premise and then note down some linking ideas and areas of development. If your idea is big enough you'll have plenty of areas for development. If it isn't, if you can only see one linear plot, you may have a short story – or possibly a novella – on your hands.

In a short story the problem the character is faced with has to be easily resolved – in a novel it can't be easily resolved, it needs to have the capacity to get more complex and to allow plenty of opportunities for the character to develop and change.

Theme

One of the major themes of Passing Shadows is second chances. It's handy to have a theme when you're writing a short story, but it's even more useful in a novel because your subplots can also echo the main theme.

For example, in Passing Shadows my theme was echoed, both by what was happening to the human characters and also what was happening to the animal characters. Their stories, although obviously different, were held together by one theme.

As in short story writing, knowing your theme before you start can help you a great deal. Don't worry if you don't know it. Hopefully it will emerge as you go along. Once it is clear in your mind it will help you with your cutting and revision.

Genre

Just as you will know which market you are targeting before you begin a short story, so you should have an idea of the genre of your novel before you start.

Are you writing a thriller, a romance, or an adventure story? You will need to know this when you approach an agent or publisher and in my experience the sooner you know this the easier it will be, both to write and sell your novel.

If you don't have a genre in mind, you might fall into the trap of writing a cross genre novel. It's fine to write a thriller with some romance in it, or a romance with some thrilling bits in it (perhaps I should rephrase that), but be careful that you don't end up with a novel stuck halfway between two genres.

They are difficult to sell because they are difficult to market. Where will your book fit in the bookshop, and how will your agent present it to a publisher? It's much easier for an agent to say, "I have this exciting new thriller by a great new novelist," than it is for them to say, "I have this exciting new romance cross adventure cross fantasy book by a great new novelist."

Once you are established you can probably get away with cross genre, but I'd advise a new novelist to try and stick to a genre if possible. It is exactly the same principle as a short story writer targeting a market.

Timescale

It's not a bad idea to work out the timescale of your novel before you begin. This may be tied up with genre. For example, if you're writing a saga then you'll naturally cover a longer time span, many years or perhaps the entire lifespan of your characters. If you're writing a thriller then you may only cover a short time span, perhaps the time it takes for the police to capture a serial killer. Likewise, a romance may only cover a short time period. How long does it take to fall in love?

But just because you're writing a novel you don't have to cover a long time span. You can set your entire novel over one day if you wish. It may be one day in the life of one character or it may be one day in the life of several. There are many novels with very short time spans, A Morning at the Office, by Edgar Mittelholzer, is a very good example.

As in a short story, you can of course use flashback to give your reader information that takes place outside of the timescale of the novel. But don't use too much flashback for the same reasons you wouldn't use it in a short story. It can hold up the action and detract from what is happening in the present.

For me, one of the major differences between a short story and a novel is the flexibility you have with time. If you only have a couple of thousand words at your disposal you can't dart around too much in time – you'll confuse your reader. If you have 90,000 words, you have much more scope. You don't even need to start at the beginning. You can start at the end or in the middle or wherever else you choose.

One of the joys of writing a novel is that you can play with time. If you want to see this in action, then I'd recommend The Time Traveller's Wife by Audrey Niffenegger. It's an education, not just in time but in structure.

To plot or not

If you have read my Short Story Writer's Toolshed you will know I don't plot my short stories in advance. I use the organic method of letting the story grow from the characters, see below.

It's possible to do this when writing a novel, but it's harder. If you are new to novel writing, it's not a bad idea to have a synopsis. How much you need to know will depend on you. I know writers who work from a 500 word synopsis, which is barely more than an overview, and I know writers who have a detailed 20,000 word synopsis including a chapter by chapter breakdown of their story.

Working to a detailed synopsis

The beauty of working like this is that you are unlikely to run out of story half way through. You already know the twists and turns of your novel and you know you have enough plot.

You will know what happens in each chapter, have a rough idea of scenes and probably know whose viewpoint each scene will be in too.

Some might say there is less spontaneity in this type of writing and perhaps there is, but just because you have a detailed synopsis, it doesn't mean you have to stick to it rigidly. There is still room for your characters to surprise you.

Incidentally, if you are lucky enough to have interested an agent or publisher on the strength of three chapters and a synopsis then you can still deviate a little from your synopsis. They are aware that writing is not an exact science!

Letting your story grow from characters

If you decide not to have a detailed plot but to let your novel grow from your characters and the conflicts you have given them, then you might run into more problems. You may end up in a plot cul-de-sac and not know how to find your way out. You will probably have to do a lot more cutting and editing. It will probably take far longer to write.

The advantage of writing like this though, in my opinion, is that it is far more exciting. I have heard writers say that they love writing their books because they want to see what happens next. And for me, this is part of the joy of writing.

There is another often overlooked advantage of this method of writing. Yes, you might do far more work than you need to, but you will have written so much about your characters that you'll probably know them extremely well. So it isn't really wasted time, it's part of getting to know your 'people'.

Passing Shadows ended up being 90,000 words but I wrote in the region of 300,000 to get to that final 90,000.

And I have to say I don't regret a minute of it. It was a joy to write.

Summary of Differences

- Short story ideas tend to focus on a single problem or incident which can be easily resolved.
- A short story idea can be quite linear; a novel idea can expand in more than one direction.
- The stakes are higher for the characters in novels than short stories.
- Generally, short stories take place over a shorter timescale, an afternoon or a day.
- There is a lot more scope for jumping around in time in a novel. In a short story too much jumping around in time will confuse the reader.

Shelf Two

Setting

Regardless of the amount of planning and plotting you do, one of the things you seriously need to think about before you start writing your novel is where you are going to set it.

Setting isn't nearly as important a factor when you're writing short stories. You can set a short story in a kitchen and it isn't necessary to tell your reader much about it, maybe it's big enough for a table and chairs and has lots of fridge magnets depicting your character's travels. You are going to need a heck of a lot more detail than this in a novel. Not all at once, I hasten to add, but you need to build setting in a novel, layer by layer, otherwise your characters will appear to be moving through a vacuum.

One of the biggest mistakes I made was to forget this when I started writing longer fiction. "Where are they?" my editor would shout. "The setting is invisible."

But what about the bigger picture – the town or city? It's possible to set a short story in a place you have never visited and for it still to sound authentic. I have sold several stories set in places I've never been. I have researched them and that's been enough.

It's possible to research settings for novels without actually going there yourself. But it's harder because you will need to know the place quite well. Your characters are going to spend a lot of time there. If you plan to set a novel in London for example and you mention specific areas, you are going to need to know them in detail.

If you don't, there's a possibility that a reader who does know the place well will be able to tell – and they may well write to your publisher and comment on it. Which brings me on to a question I am often asked.

Should you set your novel in a real place?

Personally I think it's a great idea to set a novel (or a short story) in a real place. I love reading novels set in places I know. It enhances my enjoyment of the story. However, like most of us, I find it irritating if the author has made a lot of mistakes about the setting. Either with details of layout or even something as tenuous as the current 'feel' of a place. Sometimes it's obvious that a writer is using a location they haven't visited recently.

For example, my home town of Bournemouth used to be referred to as the retirement capital of England and was known as a sleepy seaside town. It hasn't been either of these things for some years. It's more like the hen and stag night capital of England on a weekend, these days. It is obviously still a seaside town, but there is nothing sleepy about it! If I was reading a contemporary novel set in Bournemouth I would expect it to reflect the place as it is now – not how it used to be. Otherwise it wouldn't ring true.

I think that this is probably the key to using a real setting. Your story must ring true. You must have authenticity, and for me this means that if you are using a real place, you must have current relevant knowledge of it. Not just what it looks like and how it's laid out, but the sound and smell and feel of it too.

So if you do use a real place, should you name it?

It's fine to have your characters living in a suburb of Bournemouth, but it's probably wise not to give them a real address, in case you upset the people who do actually live there.

Generally a good tip would be to use real place names for big places, i.e. large towns and counties, and make them up for smaller towns or villages. This way, your reader can get a good picture of your location without you having to be too specific.

I set my second novel, Helter Skelter, in the Purbecks. The location I used for the show jumping stables was real, but I made up a name for it. There were also scenes set in Swanage, which I called Knollsey. This was based on Thomas Hardy's fictitious name for the place, but with a slightly different spelling. I think we can all learn from Hardy's approach, which was to reinvent place names, many of which are now well known, for example, Casterbridge was his name for Dorchester.

Maps

If you are using real places then you can use real maps to work out how long it will take your characters to get around. If you are using made up places then it's not a bad idea to create your own maps.

If you have created an imaginary village in the Purbecks and your characters travel to Birmingham, as mine do in Helter Skelter, then you'll need to know how long their journey will be.

But you might also want to use maps for smaller creations, for example if your characters live in a show jumping stables, as mine did, I needed to know the layout of the place because I needed to make sure I was consistent.

This isn't so important in short stories because chances are your characters are only going to be in one or two settings and they aren't so likely to revisit settings. It might sound really obvious, but if you've created a beautiful house and in one scene your character turns left to the bathroom and in another he turns right, your reader is likely to be confused.

Either use a house you know well, that way you'll have the layout fixed firmly in your head, or draw some floor plans. The floor plans used on property seller's websites are a good place to start.

Continuity is very important in a longer piece of fiction and it's quite good fun creating layouts and maps of where your characters live. You might even find out things about them that you didn't already know – the devil is in the detail as they say – which brings me on to my next point, how much detail should you use?

Settings for short stories and novels – on a technical level

Whether you're creating a setting for a short story or a setting for a novel it is no longer acceptable to simply paste in long and detailed (and possibly tedious) descriptions.

You'll need to brush stroke in your setting and it should be interweaved alongside characterisation and plot. If we use art as an analogy, I think that creating a setting for short stories is like painting in miniature, you need a tiny dab of paint here and there, while creating a setting for a novel is like having a whole great canvas at your disposal. You can splash the paint around a bit more, but just because you have a big canvas you cannot afford to waste it. You must still use it wisely. Don't waste paint!

Viewpoint and settings

I also feel strongly that your setting should be revealed through the viewpoint of your character/s. I like to see a place through a character's eyes, have it coloured by their memories. Here is an example from Helter Skelter. Vanessa, the main character, is anticipating her first glimpse in years of the fairground where she was brought up.

By the time she got to the front she was high on adrenaline, her breath catching in anticipation of her first glimpse of the fair. She stopped so sharply that a man walking behind cannoned into her.

Someone had altered the skyline. It should have been bumped with fairground rides, the big wheel, the roller coaster and the domed red and yellow roof of the helter-skelter. Instead, on the hillside where the fair should have been, she could see a gleaming white block, its windows golden eyes in the setting sun.

Although the fairground has gone, the reader sees it through Vanessa's eyes, as it would have been and as it is now.

Here is another example a little later. This is a mix of imaginary place (Kane's Funfair) with real place, Swanage Bay.

Vanessa blinked. It would be all right. In a minute she'd realise she'd taken a wrong turn and feel giddy with relief. She'd backtrack and come out in a different place and there on the hill would be the golden wrought-iron archway and neon sign proclaiming that you'd reached Kane's Funfair, 'the best funfair in the world.' She leaned on the railings that overlooked the sea and took several deep breaths of salt air. The tide was in, lapping at the stone wall, boats bobbed in the harbour and seagulls swooped above the greyish sea. Beside her a painted sign offered Dorset Belle cruises and trips to Brownsea Island and a ferry service to Poole.

Eventually she turned again to look at the alien view across the bay. There was no mistake, she was in the right place, but they were gone, the fairground, Nanna Kane, Izzy, Garrin, all gone.

The details of the sign offering cruises and trips to Brownsea Island are real. When I was researching the novel I actually stood at the point where Vanessa would have stood. I walked in her footsteps to make sure I got it right.

So to summarise, your setting will need to be authentic and relevant to the time you are writing about. Details should be threaded through the narrative so the setting is clear but not laboured, and don't forget that viewpoint is a great tool. A setting that is one character's nightmare could be another character's paradise.

Summary of Differences

- You may not have to let your readers even know which part of the country you are in when writing a short story. It can even be advantageous to let your readers fill in the blanks. In a novel you will need to be much more specific about your setting.
- You will also need to know your setting well for your novel. Don't rely on having been there once twenty years ago. Research what the place is like currently.
- You are unlikely to need to create maps of the settings in your short story. In a novel this can be very useful and an integral part of the planning.
- In both short stories and novels the setting will need to be 'seen' via your characters' viewpoints.

Shelf Three

Characters and Viewpoint

Characters are at the heart of any story, whatever its length. Without them there would be no story.

Is there a difference between short story characters and novel characters?

Yes there is – and in a nutshell, it's development. Here's how it works. While it may be possible to have characters you don't know very well in a short piece of fiction because you are not spending much time with them, in a novel you will need to know your characters inside out. If you don't they will, at best, fade off the page and at worst, be so insipid no one will care about them at all.

Characters' names

Have you ever noticed how in a novel you usually find out the character's full name fairly swiftly? In a short story, their first name is enough. If the story is in first person, often you won't know their name at all. And this is fine.

What do characters look like

Short Story

It's possible to leave a short story character's appearance entirely up to the reader. Although it's nice to have the odd detail, tall, short, blue-eyed, or blonde.

Novel

It's possible to leave a novel character's appearance entirely up to the reader too – but it's not nearly so usual to do this – and personally I like to know what the characters look like when I'm reading a novel. I like to know at least a bit anyway.

In a short story it's sufficient to mention what a character looks like – in brief – and then move on. In a novel you can't do this. You can't mention that your character has green eyes on page one and then expect your reader to remember. You need to reinforce this periodically. I don't mean you should mention they have green eyes every couple of pages, by the way – you need to be subtle. This applies to other characteristics too. For example, if it's important that your reader knows your character is short sighted then you might start off with them looking for their glasses in chapter one and have them missing an optician's appointment in chapter four.

So how do you develop characters for a novel?

We all have different ways. Some writers will know their people pretty well before they even begin page one.

They will have character charts, lists of character traits, family trees, descriptions and possibly even pictures of their characters. Some writers like to get to know them as they go along. And some will do a combination of both.

Whatever you do, you will probably find it useful to have some form of written record. Here are some practical ways of both creating characters and keeping track of them, and we're also going to touch on viewpoint.

Using index cards for characters

This was not my original way of keeping track – I used to use lists – but I've found index cards are the most helpful. I use the bigger cards, 6" x 4" as opposed to 5" x 3" as you can fit more on them. The character's full name goes on the top, alongside their date of birth.

Trial and error taught me that it was a lot more useful to keep a note of a character's date of birth than their age. That way, if you need to change a time line you've got a point of reference.

If I'm writing a short story I rarely know much detail of a character's physical appearance. If I'm writing anything longer, i.e. serial, novella or novel, I need to know a lot.

So the next thing I'll put on my character card would be a brief description, i.e. height, eye colour, hair colour, distinguishing features, e.g. nose that tilts upwards, resulting in the nickname 'turnip'. Three or four personality traits, e.g. loves bargains, can't pass a charity shop without going in for a rummage. I'll also probably put the character's relationship to main character, e.g. mother.

Using visual prompts

I don't go into too much detail physically because my next step is to find a photograph that roughly matches my character description. I find it's much more useful to have a visual image of a character than it is to have a list of visual prompts. That way I can fix their appearance in my mind and it's easier to imagine how they move around and add the smaller details that bring characters to life.

Personally, I find it's a lot better to use pictures of real people, cut from magazines. By real people, I mean, not celebrities or obviously posed shots for advertising features, although the latter can sometimes work.

Obviously, I don't use the 'real' person verbatim; I am only using the visual of that person. And this will be viewed through the filter of my perception so it's likely to change as I write. My perception of their hair colour may not be the same as theirs.

It's quite interesting how as we write our characters come alive and we add details to them that weren't in the original photos. Sometimes I find that if I refer back to my original photos of characters at the end of a novel they bear little resemblance to the character they've become in my mind's eye.

This is for me, how fictitious characters can grow out of 'real' people.

Fears and ambitions

As my story evolves and I learn more about my characters I add bits to their card. I may add things like a fear of spiders, or a secret ambition to be on reality television, anything that crops up as I write. Motivation is particularly important as it will dictate what my characters will and will not do.

A practical use

Using index cards means you can keep all your characters in a box in alphabetical order on your desk or close to your writing space. Or you could get the relevant characters out on view while you're writing scenes about them. This can help fix a visual image until they are firmly established in your mind. It's also extremely helpful if you use a character for more than one novel.

Cardboard cut outs

If you are writing a plot driven novel, then your characters should fit the plot you have lined up for them. But they must still appear real. Have you ever read a novel where the characters seemed two dimensional or where the story was spoilt because you thought they were unlikely to behave as they did? This is usually because the writer hasn't developed them sufficiently.

I also occasionally find when I'm writing my own longer fiction that a character hasn't 'come alive' for me. They feel a little 'unbelievable'. This can usually be remedied by further development.

Sometimes I realise I have made them too perfect and giving them a flaw will balance them up or sometimes they are too black and need to be lightened. After all, no character should be all good or all bad.

Make sure your characters are suitable for the plot you have in mind for them. A shy retiring type will probably not decide to form a rock band and go on a world tour.

It always amuses me when soap characters are given complete personality changes in order to fit certain plot lines that the writers have planned for them. A soap, by its nature, has to provide continuous drama over many years. I am not knocking soaps, far from it, but writing a novel is different. The characters should be suitable for your plot line. It's fine for characters to surprise your reader, in fact it's great if they can, but if your reader starts shaking their head and saying, 'no, that character would never have done that,' then you have failed as a writer.

Interviewing characters?

I have found that a very good way of developing characters is to interview them outside the novel. Or give them an extra scene which isn't in the novel. For example, in my book, Helter Skelter, I wrote a scene about my anti-hero, Richard, attending his father's funeral as a child and not being allowed to cry.

This didn't appear in the novel but it gave me some insight into why he was so emotionally cold towards his wife, Vanessa.

Monologues

You might also want to write a monologue for your character – in the same way that actors would do when creating characters for the stage. It's an excellent way to get under their skin and into their voice.

Flaws

Don't forget that it's the flaws that can often bring your characters to life most effectively. I love the fact that Val McDermid created a hero, Tony Hill, in her Wire in the Blood series, who is impotent. This would never have crossed my mind – it is immensely daring and I think it works very successfully, partly because it makes him so vulnerable.

Characters' families

Another major difference between characters in short stories and characters in novels is their families. In a short story it's not necessary for a character to have a family at all – we are spending a moment or perhaps an afternoon with them. The reader probably won't want or need to know.

In fact this is one of the problems novelists often have when they start to write short stories – they want to introduce brothers, sisters, best friends etc. There is no room for them in a short story unless they have direct relevance to the plot. In a short story they should be cut or dispensed with swiftly or simply not mentioned.

In a novel the reader will want to know about them. Unless your character is a complete enigma (and this is what you are trying to achieve) he or she will have family, friends and a history. They must have a past.

Character's jobs

In a short story the reader won't want to know what your character's job is unless it's relevant to the plot. You won't necessarily have to mention their job at all.

In a novel the reader will think it odd if they don't have a job because they will be spending a lot more time with them. Your character's career or lack of career is almost certainly going to have to be part of the story. If it isn't, you are going to have to give it at least a passing mention.

How do I keep characters under control?

This is probably the opposite problem of under developed characters. If your characters are wandering off and doing things you hadn't planned for them, then it's usually because you've developed them so well they have minds of their own. Fantastic. Well done. My personal experience of this one is to let them get on with it. You'll often end up with a much better novel.

How many viewpoints can you use in a novel?

If you are writing a short story it's hard to use more than one viewpoint – there simply isn't the space. In a novel you have the freedom to use more than one.

Do proceed with caution though. If you give all your characters the same amount of viewpoint your reader could end up wondering who the main character is supposed to be. You should know who your main character is and they should have the lion's share of the viewpoint. At least they should when you start out on the novel writing journey.

All rules can be broken when you have sufficient skill and experience to break them confidently.

How do I decide who the main character is?

If you're trying to decide on your main character – then ask yourself whose story it is? This is also very useful when you're deciding through whose eyes a scene should be written in. Ask yourself, through whose eyes will this scene be the most effective?

For example, in my novel Passing Shadows, which was set in an animal sanctuary, I wrote a scene where a child, Ben, wanders into the kennel of a dangerous dog.

This scene had to be written through Ben's eyes, in order to achieve maximum tension and emotional impact.

Using the viewpoint character who will achieve the most tension and emotional impact is quite a good rule of thumb to follow.

Summary of Differences

- Novel characters need a full name, for example, Vanessa Hamilton. Short story characters don't. Nessa is fine.
- Characters in short stories don't necessarily need jobs or families or best friends or pasts. Characters in novels do need them or they will appear undeveloped and unlikely.
- The physical characteristics of the people in your short stories can be left out or to the reader's imagination if you prefer. It's unlikely that you can do this with every character in a novel though. The visual is more important.
- Short stories tend to be told via a single viewpoint, i.e. – the main character's viewpoint. Novels can be told through several viewpoints, although you should still have a main character.

Shelf Four

Dialogue

On Shelf Three of the Tool Shed we looked at characters. We looked at how to create them, how to keep track of them and how to make sure they came alive. Dialogue is a very important part of characterisation. I once heard it said that just as you can't tell what a person is truly like until they open their mouths, you can't judge a character until you hear them speak.

Your characters will reveal aspects of their personality through what they say. Not just in the details of their conversations but also through the way that they speak. One of the biggest mistakes a new novelist can make is to give all of their characters exactly the same voice.

While it may not matter too much if you give all the characters the same voice in a short story – although I'd advise against it – in a novel it is important that your characters don't all sound exactly the same.

If they do it will be instantly noticeable. There is much more dialogue in a novel. There also tend to be more characters. You want your reader to care about them and believe in them.

The purpose of dialogue

In both short stories and novels dialogue needs to move the plot forward. Your characters should never be sitting around having idle conversations.

But dialogue isn't just about moving on the plot. Dialogue should also characterise. And this is where you really can go to town in a novel. Your characters should be much more developed in a novel than they'd need to be in a short story.

You should know their ages, their personality traits, their backgrounds, for example, what type of school did they go to, how much education did they have, and where were they brought up? All of these things will help you to determine how they speak.

Consider how your character might react to being given bad news. What would he or she say?

Example one

"You're joking – bleeding 'eck you're not joking, are you, mate?"

Example two

"Oh my goodness, I can't believe it. It's not possible."

OK, so these are quite extreme examples, but you get the idea. Your characters' vocabulary will very much depend on who they are.

How do I give my characters different voices?

The short answer to this is that you should know them extremely well. As well as knowing their background, consider aspects of their personality. Are they very impatient and always rushing around? In which case they might speak very quickly, or they might never have time to finish a sentence.

Do you have two characters who know each other so well that they can finish each other's sentences?

Is your character verbose or ponderous or uncertain? All of these personality traits will affect the way they speak.

Example

"I'm – er – um – er not sure where I am. I – er – um don't suppose you could – er – um - point me in the right direction, could you?"

"Sure can. Take the right hand turn, then second left, then onto the roundabout, then straight across, then over the railway bridge by The Red Lion. Then run along there for about half a mile. Are you with me so far?"

"Er – um – er – actually, I'm – er - not. Could you go back to the second left bit, please?"

The above is obviously a bit too much. If your characters spoke like this throughout the novel, the reader would probably get tired of it very swiftly. Less is more. You don't need to translate your characters' dialogue literally to the page. You need to show a representation of it, which brings me nicely onto dialect.

Should I use dialect?

Generally speaking I would say no – don't reproduce dialect on the page. I know that some novelists do use it with great success, but they are usually well established writers. And it takes a great deal of skill to use dialect effectively.

It is also risky. As a reader if I pick up a novel and the pages are littered with dialect I would be put off. Unless I knew the author I would probably put the book back down again. So why take the risk?

If you must use dialect, then do so sparingly. I think it's OK to have the occasional dropped h in a novel. And naturally your characters can use colloquialisms. What you can also do, and personally I think this is far more effective, is to write your character's dialogue in distinctive patterns of speech.

Different parts of the British Isles have different speech patterns. If your character is a Dorset teenager, he will have a very different pattern of speech to a Glaswegian teenager.

Even characters in the same family have different voices. There's a very good example of this in The Bad Mother's Handbook by Kate Long where grandmother, mother and daughter sound subtly but distinctly different. Also look at The Help by Kathryn Stockett for a great example of how to use dialect sparingly but very effectively.

Age of character

As we discussed in The Short Story Writer's Toolshed the age of your character will also make a big difference to their voice.

Here is an extract from my novel, Passing Shadows, between Maggie, who owns the animal sanctuary and her young godson, Ben. Mickey is Maggie's dog.

"Is it okay if I take a dog out, Auntie Maggie?"

"What's wrong with Mickey?"

"We've been out already, but he doesn't like the frost on his paws. It makes him go all skiddy."

"Okay then, but not on your own. I'll come with you if you hold on a minute."

A child and an adult will naturally have different voices. Children may make up words that don't exist, for example, skiddy, and depending on the child and their mood they may be deferential or defiant.

It's harder to get your characters speaking in different voices when they are similar to each other in background and age. When I am writing a novel I have a reasonably clear picture of each character in my mind. However, this may not be as clear when I begin. I find my characters develop and grow as I go through the novel.

Therefore, one of the things I do when I am editing is to go back through each character's dialogue and check that it sounds like them.

The following are some of the questions I will ask myself:

Does this character have a favourite word or phrase?
For example, 'actually,' or 'not on your nelly' or 'let's get this straight.'

These are fairly random examples, but you can probably picture the type of person who might say them. Does this character have a favourite term of endearment, for example, *'love'* or *'pet'* or *'darling'*?

Does this character have a favourite curse or admonishment?
If you try to keep some words or phrases exclusive to certain characters, it will go a long way to giving them different voices. If you have developed your characters sufficiently to begin with, then you will probably find that this has happened naturally.

Bad language

I am often asked how acceptable bad language is in a novel. As in a short story, it will depend very much on your market.

My advice is that you need to remain true to your characters, but bear your intended audience in mind. There are several ways of getting around this. If your intended audience will accept swearing, and there shouldn't usually be a problem with adult novels like, for example, thrillers, then let your characters swear.

If your market won't accept swearing, then you could try using a substitute word that isn't so likely to cause offence.

If a word like *'flaming'* or *'blinking'* or *'blooming'* really won't make a suitable replacement for the word you had in mind – and it's surprising how often they do, check out the soaps if you don't believe me – then you may need to use reported speech.

One of the following might well work for you:

- He cursed violently.
- Her language turned the air blue.
- I heard a stream of expletives.

To summarise, when you're creating characters have a think about how they speak before you begin writing. In this way you are much more likely to end up with three dimensional people.

Summary of Differences

- There is a lot more dialogue pro rata in a novel than in a short story, so it's essential to get it right. Your reader may not notice if your characters have the same voices in a short story – in a novel they certainly will.
- Your reader will probably be more forgiving with regard to dialect in a novel, although don't overdo it. If you use dialect and phonetic speech in a short story don't use more than the merest smattering. It is enough to 'suggest' patterns of speech in a short story.
- You can probably be more relaxed about swearing in a novel i.e. if the characters need to swear then let them. With short stories you need to be a little more careful. Swearing is probably ok for literary mags, but not for women's magazines.

Shelf Five

The First Page and Beyond

One of the things I discovered when I switched between writing short stories and novels was that one of the biggest differences between the two was the opening few paragraphs. When you're writing a short story, all you need is a good hook. You don't need to worry about the end too much – you can develop everything from the beginning.

So it stood to reason that novels were the same, weren't they? Oh no, they weren't - so I discovered after I'd tried writing several different openings for my first novel. Or at least they weren't for me.

What should be on the first page?

I have since done a lot of research. I've studied the first pages of novels written by best selling writers and debut novelists alike and I've compiled my own list of ingredients of what should be on the first page of a novel. Here it is:

Good writing

This is probably obvious, but I thought I'd mention it in passing. If you want to sell your novel then your first page is a bit like a shop window. An editor should take a look and then want to know more, so the writing should be first class, as should the presentation. Make absolutely certain there are no editing or typing mistakes.

A hook

There must be enough of a hook to make the reader want to turn the page and indeed – get past the first paragraph. This does not have to be dramatic. That will depend on the type of book you're writing, but you should try to engage the reader immediately. I find the best way to do this is to have something happening, preferably some physical action, which must be relevant to the story. For example, if you're writing a crime story, then the natural place to start is with the crime, perhaps the discovery of a body or a burglary.

At least one character

You should probably introduce a character on the first page. This won't necessarily be the main character, but it usually *is,* or it's someone closely connected to them. If it isn't, you should have a good reason.

Place

Whilst the setting doesn't have to be spelt out, and this is often not possible, there should probably be some indication. You don't need a lot; a few details that you can build on later is sufficient, for example, are your characters outside, indoors, in a city, in the countryside, on a plane, etc.

Time

Is your novel contemporary or historical? It's a good idea to indicate this fairly early on. Otherwise your reader will make assumptions which they'll possibly have to alter later.

Genre

We should also be able to tell the genre of the novel very quickly. Not necessarily from the first page, but do begin in the style in which you are likely to continue. If the novel is humorous, you might not necessarily have an hilarious event on the first page, but the genre should be reflected in the style of writing.

Dialogue

Not all first pages contain dialogue. For example, first person novels often don't need it, but it isn't a bad idea to introduce dialogue quickly. The sooner the reader hears your characters speak, the sooner they will start to care about them. Or not – as the case may be.

Descriptions of characters

Again, these do not necessarily have to be on the first page, but if you are introducing a character without giving the reader any hint of what they look like, then the reader may well formulate their own view. If you later contradict this, i.e. the reader assumes your character has brown hair and they actually have flaming red hair there is a danger of losing reader identification.

Be subtle. There is nothing worse than having your character looking in a mirror. Indicate their appearance by the way they move or mention a detail of what they are wearing.

You will need to do these things in 250 words without it appearing in the least bit contrived. Phew! No wonder I had trouble.

The first page of a short story

Depending on how long your short story is, the first page might well equate to quite a bit of the whole thing, so this is a difficult comparison. Suffice to say that the pace will be different. A short story will develop much more quickly – you'll be in the middle of the story before you know it – and you are much more likely to have flashback on the first page of a short story than you would on the first page of a novel. In fact, my first agent once gave me some advice that I've never forgotten and which has since proved invaluable. If you start a novel and then find you have to go immediately into flashback, you are probably starting in the wrong place.

How do you know if you've started in the right place?

Unless you're experienced and/or have done a lot of planning, I don't think you can be sure you've started in the right place until you've written a lot of the novel, if not all of it.

I'd advise new novelists to write several chapters before they worry too much about editing the beginning. In fact it may even be best to write your first page last. Certainly don't spend too much time on the first page until you've written a fair chunk of the novel. It is pointless to edit and perfect something you might later discard.

Researching first pages

If you are serious about getting published, you can do a lot worse than studying the work of successful writers. Have a think about some of the books you've read and then read their first pages in isolation. See how successful authors do it.

Top tip

Concentrate on writers who have just had their debut novel published, NOT writers who have dozens of books out. You can learn a lot from established writers, but your research needs to be current. Better still, if you ever have the opportunity to look at the pre-edited first page of a novel that caught a publisher or agent's attention, then grab it with both hands. What was it that made that manuscript stand out from the piles of others the publisher received?

Beyond the first page - hooks

So, having written the perfect first page of your novel, or at least the first draft of one, where do you go from there? How do you keep your reader hooked?

One of the ways to keep the reader hooked is not to answer questions too quickly. Again, this may seem obvious, but I've read some great starts to first novels, which peter out after the first few thousand words. The writer has set up a fabulous dilemma with several unanswered questions, but has then, unfortunately made the mistake of answering them all by the end of chapter one.

You must always have unanswered questions – the moment you answer all of them, is the moment your reader stops being interested. The easiest way to illustrate this point is to go back to our crime novel. If, for example, we started with a body on page one, and by chapter seven the police and the reader are close to finding out who murdered the victim, and perhaps even have someone in mind to arrest, then it might be time for a second murder, which the suspect couldn't possibly have committed, because they are in custody.

In this way the reader is kept guessing and will continue to turn the pages. In fact, if there is one golden rule of writing a successful novel then that would be it, keep the reader turning the pages.

Chapter Endings/cliffhangers

Short stories don't have cliffhangers – novels will need them. Try to end chapters with a little hook. This does not have to be a major drama, again, it will depend on what you're writing, but you should end your chapter leaving your reader wanting more.

One of the best tips I was ever given about chapter endings was never to end with my character falling asleep, as it was likely that my reader would follow suit!

Summary of Differences

- There is a great deal of set up information on the first page of a novel. But it must appear uncontrived and it must still have a strong hook.
- The first page of a short story is lighter, pacier, thinner.
- It's rare to go into flashback on the first page of a novel. Short stories often go swiftly into flashback on the first page.
- Short stories don't have cliffhangers. Novels will need them.

Shelf Six

Development, Author Voice and Endings

On shelf six of the toolshed I want to focus on how to develop your characters and plot as you head towards the middle of your novel, and how to write the end.

We're also going to touch on author voice and have a look at some of the pitfalls that may arise when you're writing something longer and how to avoid them!

The Middle

I think that the middle of a novel can be quite difficult to write. This is probably partly psychological. Real life has kicked in; you aren't feeling quite as motivated as you were when you began. It still seems to be an awful long way to the end. You're no longer sure exactly where your story is going. Does any of this sound familiar?

It certainly happened to me. When I write a short story I barely notice the middle, I've practically written it before I've realised where I am. But of course a novel is that much longer and the middle can be a sticky patch.

The good news is that once you get past the middle it's a lot easier. You're on the downhill slope, so to speak. So what should the middle of a novel actually be doing?

Well, I think it should deepen character and plot and build up towards the three quarter mark. The middle is the time to answer some of the questions you've set up, but also give the reader some new information about characters and plot that raise more questions and gets them even more deeply involved with your story. It's a good time for subplots to develop too. Generally a sub plot, i.e. one that is running alongside (but not overshadowing) the main plot is resolved before the main plot.

Pitfalls – keeping track of characters

One of the pitfalls of writing something longer is trying to keep track of characters, particularly minor characters, what they look like, what their characteristics are etc.

As I mentioned in the characterisation section, I find the best way to do this is to keep index cards for them, which will include a picture, their date of birth and some pertinent points about their characters.

Keeping track of the story

Another pitfall of writing something longer is trying to keep track of exactly what's happened so far. In a short story you can simply read back. In a novel this isn't possible.

I've found the best way to keep track is to write a chapter summary as I go along. This will only be a couple of sentences, for example, this is the overview of the first two chapters of Helter Skelter:

Chapter one

Vanessa receives a letter from Purbeck District Council asking her to remove items of value from her daughter's grave as they are carrying out upgrades to the memorial garden. Richard tries to dissuade her from going, saying it will only stir up bad memories of the past.

Chapter two

On her way to the memorial garden, Vanessa detours to the fairground site where she was brought up and discovers it has been redeveloped into flats and Richard is the developer. Why has he never told her?

Keeping track of your novel as you write has two major advantages. One of them is that you can pinpoint exactly when events happen, particularly if you are dotting about in time. The other is that you know something *has* actually happened. It's quite easy in a novel to waffle on for a long time in a scene where there is very little action taking place.

The main character might be reflecting on events in the past, for example, but not actually doing very much now.

Voice

This is a word that is often bandied about by critics and writing tutors alike. But what does it actually mean?

It's a hard thing to define. For me, it means the way that a novel is written; style comes close, but it's a little bit more than style, it has to do with the author and how they come across. Although, these days, not many novelists, directly address the reader, '*and that, dear reader, is how the story begins,*' the author is of course there. No matter how hidden they are, their presence shines through between the lines, and this is how it should be. Otherwise all novels would feel the same.

How do you develop voice?

I think this comes with practice. When we begin to write we often model ourselves on our favourite authors. We unconsciously (or not) emulate their style. This rarely works. It's better to develop your own style. And as writers grow more confident, that is generally what happens.

The more you write, the more your own individual voice will emerge. We all write in a way that instinctively feels comfortable to us and I think that this is what becomes our voice.

It's difficult to decide if your own writing has a voice, but anyone who regularly reads your work will be able to tell you. In my writing classes we have regular writing competitions. To make it fair, students enter these anonymously by putting their stories in a folder on my desk, but after being with a class for a while and listening to their work read out, I find I can identify certain entries, because the authors have a very strong voice.

Three words that sum up voice

If I had to pick three words that sum up voice, I would say: passion; honesty; and language. When you write your first draft let it all hang out. Don't edit yourself, be passionate, be messy. But also be truthful. Our writing, our creativity, comes from deep within us. Get in touch with your inner truth. Be aware of the language you use. Be aware of how you actually say things. What words are really you? In this way, I think you will find your own voice.

Writing the end

I have written nowhere near as many novels as I have short stories, but so far I have discovered that while writing the end of a short story is hard work and very difficult to get right, finishing a novel is a joy.

I think this is because all the really hard work has gone on prior to writing the end. You have built up your characters and plot to what is (hopefully) a satisfying conclusion. You need to tie up loose ends, of course, although not necessarily all of them. Don't make your ending too neat.

Your ending needs to bring the story to a satisfactory conclusion, one that the reader might have hoped for but that is not predictable. It might be a twist. In a thriller, for example, the person you think has been carrying out the murders hasn't actually carried out all of them.

But beyond the main ending of the story, it is also not a bad idea to keep some element of surprise to the end. This could be something as simple as an unanswered question that was set up early on in the novel, and is tied up with the resolution.

My agent calls it the after eight mint effect. Coffee might be the conclusion of a meal, but the after eight mint is what really finishes it off!

Summary of differences

- Whether you are writing a short story or a novel, the middle is possibly the easiest part to get wrong. Both need to be handled with care.
- It's easy to keep track of what's happened in a short story. In a novel you will probably need some kind of system – a chapter summary or a timeline.
- It's easy to keep track of characters in a short story. In a novel you will probably need some system like index cards.
- Author voice becomes more critical in a novel. It's important that it's strong and consistent.
- It's a great deal easier to write the end of a novel than it is to write the end of a short story. Possibly because most of the hard work has been done!

Shelf Seven

Structure and Flashback

Just as structure tends to be overlooked by short story writers, I suspect that novelists also don't give it as much thought as they do to other aspects of their writing.

Yet it is a very important part of writing something longer. More so, if anything, than in a short story because a novel is that much more unwieldy. A good structure can help to make it easier to write, can strengthen it, and almost certainly will make it more readable.

So what exactly do I mean by structure?

Structure is one of those aspects of writing which you only notice when it's not working. Many novels are written with no visible structure, but that doesn't mean it isn't there. Some have more obvious ones. Here are some examples of structure:

Novels split into parts or viewpoints
Some novels are split into two or more parts and each one has a heading, for example, Part One, Part Two and Part Three, or The Beginning, The Middle, The End. There are often time gaps between them, i.e. Part One

might take place in the 70s, Part Two, the 80s and Part Three, the 90s. Or the parts may all take place in the same time period, but be from different character's points of view. These characters will need to be linked; perhaps they are sisters, or three friends. Or perhaps they are strangers, but are linked by a central event. In that way the three parts of the novel make up a cohesive whole.

Short stories split into parts or viewpoints

Using the structure of parts or viewpoints can work for short stories too, but keep it simple. Dual or, at the most, triple viewpoint is plenty, and keep them in sections, don't mix them. There are some much more subtle structures that can work in short stories that won't work in novels. For example, splitting a short story into several sections all of which begin with the same words can work very well. I once sold a short story which had five separate sections in it – each one began with the words, *it is raining.* This type of thing is generally too subtle for a novel.

Using time as a structure

As with short stories, time can also be used as the structure. There are novels which are split into sections that are headed up day and night. Or sometimes they are headed up with specific dates, which don't necessarily have to be in the right order. The Time Traveller's Wife by Audrey Niffenegger is a great example of this.

Another time structure might show past and present written in alternating chapters, for example, Chapter One begins with some dramatic scene like a kidnapping. And Chapter Two tells some of the back story that led up to the kidnapping. The novel continues with chapters alternating between the past and the present.

While this is a great structure to use, do be careful, as there is a danger that the reader may be so interested in what is happening in the present that she won't want to know about the back story, or possibly vice versa!

Each section must have its own hooks and cliff hangers and the pace must be sustained.

Diary structure

I probably don't need to say too much about diary structures, but they can work extremely well. We all remember Bridget Jones's Diary and some of us will remember The Secret Diary of Adrian Mole, aged 13 ¾.

Letter structure

Again, this is self-explanatory; the novel is divided up into letters through which the story is revealed. Many fine novels have been written entirely in the form of letters.

Most of the above structures can be used in short and longer fiction, but prologues and epilogues tend to be specific to novels.

Using a prologue

Generally used only in novels (or at least I've never seen one in a short story) a prologue is a piece of writing, usually short, about an event or events that happen before the novel begins. The event is often dramatic, and must of course be significant to the story. It is not necessary for the reader to grasp the significance of the event straight away.

Prologues tend to be headed up with a date so the reader knows when the event took place.

Some interesting points about prologues

I have noticed that a lot of new writers decide to use a prologue, perhaps because they are good fun to write.

However, I once did a mini-survey amongst my students and discovered that most of them didn't like *reading* a prologue and would often skip it if they came across one in a novel. A lot of editors and publishers also dislike prologues. So perhaps this is also worth bearing in mind. It's often possible to write the information you need to convey as flashback instead of as a prologue.

To be truthful the only reason you should be writing a prologue is if there is no other way of getting the information into your novel.

Epilogues

I suspect that readers don't have the same trouble with epilogues – mostly because by the time they reach the end of the book they care about the characters and want to know what happens to them next.

Epilogues are often used to show events that take place after the novel has finished, they can tie up loose ends and let the reader know how their favourite characters ended up.

Flashback

It is even harder to write a novel without using flashback than it is to write a short story, because at some point your reader is going to need to know information and back story about your characters.

However, do use flashback with caution. As I've already mentioned it's not a good plan to use flashback on the first page of a novel.

If you are going to use flashback at the beginning of your novel you should have a very good reason. You do not, of course, need to write your novel in chronological order at all. If you're writing a relationship story you may want to start with the hero and heroine already together and then pop in a chapter later in the novel which shows them meeting for the first time.

Whatever you decide to do with flashback, the same rules apply to novels as they do to short stories. Do not divert the reader from the main thrust of the action for too long. There is a danger they will stop reading. And make sure the reader is not confused about exactly where they are in the story.

Summary of differences

- Prologues and epilogues are not used in short stories; they are devices for novels.
- Very subtle structures don't tend to work in novels; they are more suited to short stories.
- It's much easier to experiment with time and viewpoint in a novel than it is in a short story where you don't have the same space for development. But it can be done in both – if you're skilful.
- Flashback on the first page of a short story is fine. Flashback on the first page of a novel is probably not.

Shelf Eight

Editing and Revision

Editing and revision – they sound like hard work, don't they? And there's no doubt about it, they are, but it's in the process of editing and revising that your best writing emerges.

Or at least this is my opinion. When you edit you remove anything superfluous, that's scenes and chapters as well as words, and you sharpen the sense and also, I believe, the beauty of what you are writing.

I have spoken to writers who refuse to edit their work at all. "That's how it is," they say. "That's how I wrote it and that's how it's staying." Or they might say, "But I particularly like that bit."

I even once heard a writer say, "I know that part of my novel isn't as good as the rest but frankly I need the words. It's the perfect length. If I cut it then I'll have to write 5000 more words."

None of these are good reasons not to edit. Why would you want to keep sections of your novel that aren't relevant and aren't moving the story forward? In my experience, most pieces of writing can be improved greatly with revision.

Editing short stories

Editing short stories is a lot easier than editing novels. Perhaps because the pure scale of the job is that much bigger with a novel. But let's just take a quick look at the similarities between the two – and the differences.

When you edit a short story, you might do some of the following:

- Ensure the opening paragraph is eye catching and has sufficient hook to make the reader want to read on.
- Cut superfluous words and phrases.
- Make sure the characters are real and not cardboard cut outs.
- Make sure the dialogue sounds authentic.
- Check the plot works and is not contrived or predictable.
- Give the reader enough setting to be able to visualise where characters are.
- Make sure the end is not predictable, doesn't tail off, and has some resonance.
- Make sure the story fits the word length required.

Editing a novel

You will very likely need to do all the above, but in much more depth. For example:

- Make sure the opening chapter has enough pace and interest to involve the reader and draw her into the story.

- Cut superfluous scenes. If we've already experienced an event through one character's eyes, do we need to see it through another's? (We might if new, crucial information is added.)

- Are any of your characters surplus to requirements? Often, two characters in similar roles, for example, the main character's friend and her sister could be combined into one.

- Make sure your characters have different voices. Can you tell them apart without their dialogue tags or do they all sound exactly the same?

- Will the reader care about your main character and his or her problems? If you're writing about an action hero trying to save the world or a Detective Inspector trying to solve a brutal crime it shouldn't be so difficult to get the reader to identify with them. But if you're writing about ordinary people, how will you get the reader to care about them? This is very important.

- Are there any glaring plot holes? Does the plot rely on a coincidence or an unlikely series of events?

- Is your setting real, accurate and sufficiently well drawn so the reader will be able to visualise it, even if she has never been to the place where your characters live? Reading a novel with very little setting is a bit like walking through a city with blinkers on.

- Just as short stories have lengths that are dictated by the market, so does a novel. Most mainstream publishers will require a novel of between 80 and

90,000 words. If you are sending them a novel of 40,000 words or 240,000 words, they may well reject it without reading.

By the way, if you wanted any proof that first drafts can be improved, look no further. Here are some drafts of the opening paragraph of my second published novel, *Helter Skelter.*

First draft

Vanessa Hamilton bent to pick up the post from the mat and glanced at it without much interest. Ninety nine per cent of it would be for Richard. It always was. He ran a property development business from home. She didn't check the post properly until she'd unloaded the dishwasher and had another cup of coffee. And then she realised that there was a letter for her. A letter postmarked Dorset and the postmark alone was enough to send darts of ice flicking along her spine.

Hmmm, not terribly impressive for the opening of a novel, is it? Main character opens post, unloads dishwasher and has a cup of coffee – gripping stuff! The very slight hook in the final line is spoilt by being overwritten.

Later draft

Vanessa Hamilton knew as soon as she opened her eyes that it was the day she would leave her husband. Why, was harder to pinpoint. You left your husband because he had affairs, or too much to drink or because he beat you, or simply because you'd grown apart. None of these things applied to her and Richard. He was exactly the same as he'd been on the day she'd married him, eight years earlier. She was the same too. Or at least she would be once she was up, sliding into the routines of coffee, grapefruit, housework, Saturday morning things.

This is slightly better. The first line isn't bad. But sadly it deteriorates rapidly from there. It's confusing. And I was obviously determined to get the domestic detail in at the end. How exciting exactly are coffee, grapefruit and housework?

Also, it struck me that I wasn't really starting in the right place. I wanted to start with the fact that Vanessa is still grieving for her stillborn baby, not that she has married Richard on the rebound.

Final draft

Vanessa Hamilton awoke to the sound of a child's laughter. Caught between the limbo of sleep and wakefulness she shoved back the duvet and sat up in the dimness of the curtained room with a smile on her face. And then reality crashed in like a punch to the heart.

This final draft is shorter, punchier and more to the point. I doubt very much that I would have got the earlier drafts published.

Ways to cut without losing continuity

I find that it is very helpful when I'm cutting a novel to save the bits I have cut in a separate document. I may, for example, have written a whole chapter which I later cut because it's repetitive, but on page 23 of that chapter there was one vital piece of information without which the plot falls down.

Whatever's on page 23 will need to go back in somewhere else in the book, otherwise I will have one of those glaring plot holes I mentioned earlier.

Cooling down periods

I recommend that you have a cooling down period before editing your work. Write in the heat of passion, but edit with a cool head. In my experience time is the only way to get a cool head. You need to revisit your work when the words have had a chance to cool on the page. For a short story, a day or two later is fine. For a novel you will probably need to leave longer, possibly as much as a week.

If you don't have the benefit of time, try this for a novel. Write a one sentence summary for each chapter. This will help you to see if you are being repetitive and will indicate where to make cuts.

Final edits

Do these on paper not a computer screen. It's much easier to spot mistakes on paper. Also bear in mind that the ear is a better editor than the eye. Reading your work aloud can help you spot mistakes you wouldn't see on the page. Reading your work aloud is also an excellent way to make sure the rhythm is right. If a piece of work is beautifully written and edited, it will have a natural rhythm. A rhythm that you can almost dance to – try it and you'll see what I mean.

Summary of differences

- You will need a cooling off period to edit your work. This can be a day or two for a short story, but you need a longer break, maybe as much as a month for a novel.
- Do the final edits, whether for short story or novel on paper.
- Date your drafts, particularly for novels. It's a lot easier to remember which is the most current.

Shelf Nine

The Title, The Synopsis, The Blurb

Whether you are writing a short story or a novel you will need a great title. Your title is one of your selling points. For far too long I thought that titles didn't matter too much, but they do. A great title can sell a piece of work, not just to an agent or publisher but to your readers too.

So, what's a great title?

Whether you are writing short stories or novels, your title should be eye catching. It should also reflect what your fiction is about without being too general. On a practical note don't make a novel title so long that the publisher has trouble getting it on the cover. And do choose carefully if you are writing a series. You may be stuck with your title for a very long time!

Although there is no copyright on titles it is probably better if you don't have the same title as another novel currently in print. A good way to check is to type your title into Amazon and see if there are any matches. If there are, then it might be wise to think again.

Also, bear in mind that the publisher may change the title. *Helter Skelter* was originally called *The Forgiving*, which my publisher felt was too generic.

What's the difference between a short story title and a novel title?

Is there even one? Yes, I think there is. Perhaps it's a question of size. Novels are a lot bigger than short stories and maybe they need a title to reflect this. I don't mean you should use a title for your novel that is lengthy (although these can work well). I mean that you should think big in terms of words. Consider the following two lists:

Atonement	Hailstones
Obsession	Shoes
Sisters	Peanuts
Mercy	Buzzwords
Sin	Priorities
Unforgiven	Butterflies

And yes, as I'm sure you've guessed, the ones on the left are novel titles and the ones on the right are short story titles. Some of them are interchangeable, but generally speaking novel titles are much bigger. They hint at big themes and big subjects. They are deeper.

But here are some tips on finding a good title whatever you write.

Think theme

Think about your theme – one word titles tend to echo the theme, which is why they can work for either short or long fiction.

Be specific and be unusual

The more specific a title the more interesting it is. I am not especially interested in either the history of tractors or the Ukraine, but I could not resist *A Short History of Tractors in Ukrainian* as a title. The same applies to *The Secret Life of Bees.*

The Girl with the Dragon Tattoo is also a very evocative title. As is *The Boy in the Striped Pyjamas.* These titles are also visual. You'll instantly have a picture in your head. I think you'll agree that they're much more interesting than general titles like, *Fields*, or *Dreams*, or *Memories*. Not that there's anything wrong with these titles – if they're extremely relevant, but imagine that you're standing in a book shop surrounded by hundreds of titles, or flicking through an ebook store.

Which title is going to catch your attention – *Dreams* or *The Girl with the Dragon Tattoo?*

Be provocative

Being slightly provocative never hurts. *The God Delusion* is a good example of this, I think. Whatever your beliefs it certainly sticks in your mind. And this is definitely one of the things a good title should do.

Before you choose a title

Make a list of titles that stick in your mind. Ask yourself why they stick in your mind. Then think about these reasons carefully and apply the same principles to choosing your title.

Now on to writing a synopsis, which interestingly never used to apply to short story writers, but that is beginning to change.

Writing a synopsis

The thought of writing a synopsis strikes dread into many a writer's heart. But sooner or later you are probably going to need to write one.

So what exactly is meant by a synopsis? In its simplest terms, a synopsis is an overview of what happens in your novel or story, but there is a bit more to it than that. In my experience there is more than one type of synopsis, but let's concentrate first on the type you will need to send to an agent or publisher. And let's start with novels.

The selling synopsis

This tells the agent what your novel is about, but it will also need to intrigue them. A list of dry facts is not going to act as a very good selling tool. The best description I've heard of a 'selling synopsis' is 'a summary of your novel with feeling'. Or you might prefer, 'a blurb with an end'.

Why do publishers need one?

Most publishers haven't got time to read the entire novel, in the first instance. They ask for the opening chapters, which show them how you write, and a synopsis, which tells them what the novel is about and that there is enough plot to sustain the length.

What length should a synopsis be?

Lengths vary from publisher to publisher, so check this, but the current trend is towards a shorter synopsis. Many publisher and agents require a one page synopsis (about 500 words) for a novel of about 90,000 words.

How should I present it?

The synopsis should be typed in single line spacing unless the publisher specifies differently. It should also be written in third person and in present tense. It can be helpful to highlight the name of each main character as they are introduced by underlining or capitalising the text.

Do I have to give away the end?

Yes, you do, which is why it's so hard to write a good synopsis. You can and should set up questions in the rest of the synopsis though – a good synopsis should intrigue and excite the reader and make them want to read on. It should also give the tone of the novel, for example, humorous or tense.

What else should be included?

Your synopsis should introduce your MAIN characters and MAIN scenes. It should tell the publisher where the novel is set and what it is about. It does not have to include minor characters, although it might include a sub plot. It might also include the theme of your novel.

An example synopsis

Let's look at how this works in more detail. Here is the beginning of my synopsis for my second novel, Helter Skelter.

Helter Skelter is a contemporary love story set in a show jumping yard on the beautiful Purbeck coast.

You don't have to begin a synopsis like this but it isn't a bad idea to introduce your story by telling the publisher what type of novel it is and where it is set. You should then go on to introduce your main characters and the beginning of the plot.

Being a kept, suburban wife is a far cry from the life <u>Vanessa Hamilton</u> once had, growing up and working in a fair, but as time goes on an emptiness grows in her and she realises that in turning her back on her past, she has *also lost something of herself. During the eight years of her marriage to property developer, <u>Richard</u>, she hasn't seen <u>Aunt Izzy</u>, who brought her up or <u>Nana Kane</u>, who owned the fairground, or <u>Garrin Tate,</u> the man she was desperately in love with until she became pregnant at twenty and their child was tragically stillborn. When the ache becomes unbearable, she leaves Richard to go in search of Garrin because she knows she will never be happy until she lays the ghosts of her past.*

Note how important characters are introduced by their full name, although less important ones might not be named at all.

You will then go on to tell the agent how the novel develops, what crisis points there are. This is how Helter Skelter develops:

Vanessa finds a block of flats on the old fairground site and is shocked to learn that Nanna Kane died shortly after she left, leaving the fairground to Garrin. She is also stunned to discover that the land was bought and developed by her husband's firm. She tracks Garrin down to the yard where he trains both horses and people and has established a reputation as a brilliant, but ruthless instructor.

Garrin has not forgiven Vanessa and he is not pleased to see her. However, they do spend a passionate night together. The following morning he throws her out and Vanessa realises, too late, that he was motivated not by love, but revenge. Shortly afterwards Vanessa discovers that she is pregnant once more. She knows now that she is still in love with Garrin and she dreams that he will soften towards her when he finds out she is carrying their child.

As I've already mentioned, you will need to give away the end in your synopsis. You can't leave the agent or publisher to guess. This is one good reason to finish a novel before you send out your submission package. I find that very often I won't know the end until I've written it.

Also, it isn't a bad idea to mention the themes of your novel in a synopsis:

Forgiveness and revenge are the running themes as the story reaches its dramatic conclusion.

One of the most helpful tips I've been given about writing a synopsis is to imagine that you are telling a friend what your book is about – this will be the bones of your synopsis, and then expand outwards from there.

I mentioned earlier that there are two types of synopsis. The other type I was referring to is a 'working synopsis'.

Working synopsis

This is a breakdown, either scene by scene or chapter by chapter, of your novel and exactly what is in it. If you are the kind of writer who plots in detail, you might find it useful to do this before you begin. The advantages of working like this is that you will then know exactly where you are going and are unlikely to run into any plot cul-de- sacs.

These kinds of synopsis tend to be much longer and much more detailed and they are a great writing tool.

Even if you don't do one in advance, they are also quite useful to do as you actually write your novel. They will help you to keep track of events, i.e. when and where they happen and make it much easier to edit later.

Writing a blurb for a novel

Traditionally, a blurb is what goes on the back cover of your novel and is used to sell it in a book shop or an online store. The prospective reader will scan the blurb to see if it catches their attention and if it does they will buy it.

Some publishers/editors will write the blurb for you, but many of them won't and I think it's a useful skill for a writer to have. No one knows the book better than you, after all. Also, it's helpful to have a blurb handy when you are trying to sell your novel to an agent or publisher.

If you think of blurbs as selling tools, it might help you to write them more easily.

What should be in a blurb?

It should entice the reader to buy the book, as well as to give enough information to tell the reader what sort of book they are buying, i.e. thriller, romance, historical. It should also introduce the main character/s and give an idea of the plot.

The following is the blurb for my novel, *Helter Skelter.*

Brought up on a seaside fairground, Vanessa knows all about what a rollercoaster ride life can be. Tragedy forces her to flee, but when she discovers that her husband, a property developer is cheating on her, she returns. But the fair has gone, the land, bought by her husband, is now covered in luxury flats. Going back can be painful but this is just the start of the Helter Skelter for Vanessa. While she feels her life is spiralling ever downwards, there are the strong arms of a passion from the past to catch her at the end.

Facts about this blurb

- It has 98 words.
- It introduces the main character by name.
- It gives us a taste of the plot.
- It gives us a taste of the setting
- We know the book is probably a romance.

It also uses strong words such as tragedy, cheating, luxury, passion. When you don't have many words at your disposal, they need to be chosen well.

Writing a blurb for your own novel, even if you have no intention of actually writing a novel at this moment, is an interesting exercise in itself as it teaches you how to focus on the bare bones of a story line. Who knows, you might be so taken with your blurb you want to write the book to find out what happens!

Writing a synopsis for a short story

This was something you probably wouldn't have needed to worry about too much once. But it's getting more common for editors of both print and online magazines to ask for them. You will also need to write them if you publish your work online yourself. So I thought I'd mention them briefly. Here are a couple of examples of short story synopses.

At Her Time of Life

Dorothy finds out it's never to late to follow your dreams, especially where horses are concerned.
(16 words)

A Souvenir from Skegness

Sarah doesn't believe in karma but when she gives up her holiday to help her sister, things certainly turn out well for her.
(23 words)

As you can see, these are very short but they are long enough to tell an editor what your story is about. Enough of synopses. Let us move on to blurbs.

Here are some short story blurbs for the same stories mentioned above.

At her Time of Life

Dorothy had never imagined she'd learn to ride a horse at her time of life: she was a grandmother after all. But when she was housesitting for a week, the docile Candy Girl proved to be just too much of a temptation.
(42 words)

A Souvenir from Skegness

When Sarah gave up her holiday plans to help out at her sister's ice cream stall in Skegness she imagined she'd also forgone the chance of any fun. But fun – and indeed romance – can turn up in the most unexpected places!
(41 words)

Interestingly, when it comes to short stories, the blurbs may actually be longer than the synopsis.

Summary of differences

- Titles for novels tend to be 'bigger' than title for short stories, both in theme and idea.
- To find a great title for either a novel or short story you will need to be specific.
- A novel synopsis is usually about a page (500 words), whereas a short story synopsis can be as little as a line.
- A novel blurb tends to be shorter than a novel synopsis.
- A short story blurb tends to be longer than a short story synopsis.
- Unless you are self publishing you will probably never need to write a blurb for a short story, but regardless of whether you are publishing your own novel or being traditionally published, you'll need to write a blurb.

Shelf Ten

Finding an Agent or Publisher

This section of the toolshed is aimed purely at novelists. You won't need an agent for short stories. You can submit them direct to your targeted market.

Let's start with the million dollar question: Do you need an agent or publisher for your novel? The short answer is no, you don't. It is possible to sell direct to your readers today.

So why bother looking for an agent or publisher at all? The short answer to this is validation.

Sending out your work

Most writers send out their work before it is really 'finished'. I know how hard it is not to – the novel is written, it has been edited and revised – why not get it out there?

The main reason is because it's probably not as 'finished' as you think. Have you left it to cool for at least a month, and then had one final read through and edit? It is amazing how often I've packaged up three chapters and synopsis and then when it's come back again a month or so later I've realised there are mistakes I simply didn't notice in the fire of my enthusiasm.

What will happen if I send out my work too soon?

It'll get rejected. Incidentally, contrary to what some authors clearly think, exactly the same thing will happen if you self publish too soon. Only in this case it will be rejected by readers. There will be no sales. Or worse, if there are sales, you may end up with bad reviews. Don't do it. Your reputation as a writer is too valuable to short change yourself.

How do I know if I'm sending out my work too soon?

Ask a like-minded writer friend to read it for you and give you feedback. If this is not possible, you might want to use a critique agency. They are not cheap, but a good one is money well spent. Get recommendations from friends/writing tutors. Use an agency that has current market knowledge in your genre. If your genre is romance you could do a lot worse than joining the Romantic Novelist Association (RNA) and using their New Writer Scheme. (This is how I first got an agent to notice my work)

OK, so you are absolutely sure you really are ready. Your books is as good as it can be, for now (an agent or publisher might require more edits later!) what's next?

Should I choose an agent or publisher?

Views vary on this, but my view is that you should try an agent first. This is for practical reasons. If you send your book to every publisher in the land and they turn you down – and then you find an agent, he or she will have nowhere left to submit your manuscript.

Where do I look for an agent or publisher?

There are the tried and trusted ways of looking through The Writers' and Artists' Yearbook or Writer's Market (if you're in the US). Agents and publishers and a brief summary of what they do are listed alphabetically.

The internet is a useful resource too. Check out Duotrope. https://duotrope.com As well as finding a reputable agent or publisher there are also websites listing ones that aren't so good, for example Preditors and Editors. www.pred-ed.com

Also check out LitFactor here: http://litfactor.com/

Incidentally, reputable agents and publishers do not advertise in writing magazines and national newspapers for prospective clients. They are already inundated with enquiries from prospective clients.

In my experience, by far the best way to find an agent or publisher is to meet them in person. I don't mean you should go and knock on their doors or invite yourself to their barbecues (although I have heard of writers doing this). I mean you should go to writing conventions or literary festivals where they are speaking – or you should join organisations pertinent to your form of writing. I've already mentioned the RNA or the RWA in the US. There is also the CWA (Crime Writers' Association) in the UK. There are numerous other writing conventions, schools and literary festivals where agents speak. See the list at the foot of this section for the UK.

Once you have listened to them speak about what they are looking for – and, if you are lucky, you might even get a chance to meet them in the bar afterwards – if you've met them in person it is far easier to approach them with your novel submission at some later date. Don't take your submission to the bar unless they suggest it. You will then be in a position to start your covering letter with the words, *Thank you for your excellent talk at Green Gables Literary Festival, it was lovely to meet you...*

What do I send to an agent or publisher?

Once you have established your target agent or publisher, read their guidelines carefully. Most require: a covering letter to include a brief biography, three chapters and a synopsis. Some will require fewer chapters or will state wordage. Some will ask you to post your work. Others will ask you to email. If you are posting it, don't forget return postage.

What should be in a covering letter?

Keep them brief. They are a professional introduction. Here is a sample:

Dear Ms Agent

Following your excellent talk at Green Gables Convention, which I enjoyed very much, I am now hoping you might consider representing me.

Please find enclosed three chapters and a synopsis of my crime thriller, The Kill, which is a novel of approximately 90,000 words.

I am new to writing but my background is in criminology. I worked as a crime scene officer for Wiltshire Police for 30 years.

The novel is complete. Many thanks for your time. I look forward to hearing what you think.

Yours sincerely

If you have done your homework and your novel is good enough your prospective agent will ask to see the rest. Send it by return of post/email. Do not wait a few months while you edit and then send it. They'll probably have forgotten all about it by then!

Can I submit to several agents or publishers simultaneously or do I have to approach one at a time?

The short answer is yes, you can send out simultaneous submissions. Many writers do because it saves time. This can get you into hot water, though, if several agents/publishers ask to see your book at the same time and they each require an exclusive right to read it – as happened recently to one of my friends.

I use the following system. If I am submitting cold, i.e. I don't know or haven't met the agent or publisher I would multi submit and I would tell them in my covering letter that I am doing so. If I have met them, I would, out of courtesy, submit only to them and I would wait until they reply before I send my proposal to the next one. This can be time consuming but at least I know I won't be caught out and most agents and publishers are very efficient.

And while we're on the subject of finding an agent or publisher, as I mentioned earlier, conferences are a great place to look. So here are a few of the conferences and festivals I personally recommend. Happy hunting.

Some writing conferences and festivals in the UK

The Winchester Writers Conference
http://www.writersconference.co.uk/

Writers' Holiday (Fishguard, Wales)
http://www.writersholiday.net/

Swanwick, The Writers' Summer School
http://www.swanwickwritersschool.co.uk/

RNA (Romantic Novelists' Association)
http://www.rna-uk.org/

CWA (The Crime Writers' Association)
http://www.thecwa.co.uk/

Wells Festival of Literature
http://www.wellslitfest.org.uk/

Some writing conferences and festivals in the USA

RWA (Romance Writers of America)
http://www.rwa.org/

Romcon
http://www.romcon.com/

Society of children's book writers and illustrators
http://www.scbwi.org/Pages.aspx/42nd-Annual-Summer-Conference

AWP (Association of Writers and Writing Programs)
www.awpwriter.org/awp_conference/

RT Booklovers Convention
http://www.rtconvention.com/

A Last Word From Me

So there you have it. You know what the tools are and I very much hope I've been helpful in showing you how to use them. The next step is practice. Learn how to use the tools effectively by writing as often as you can. Writing is like any other craft, the more you do it the better you'll get. So practice and practice and practice. If you love writing that bit will be no hardship. For me, one of the most amazing things about writing is that it's possible to get better and better. If you don't believe me, take a look back at some of your early work. I am always quite shocked when I do this. Did I really write that? More embarrassingly, did I really send it off hoping it would be published? Thank goodness publishers and agents were kind enough not to hold it against me!

And now... all that remains for me to say is, have fun, and happy writing.

If You've Enjoyed This Book...

I hope you've enjoyed this book as much as I enjoyed writing it. Why not give '*The Short Story Writer's Toolshed*' a try?

In the meantime, if you've found it useful and you'd like to 'spread the word', then here are a few ways you can do just that.

'Like' my Facebook Page

Pop along to www.facebook.com/dailydella, and click the LIKE button (up there at the top). Your 'friends' will be able to see that you're a fan, and you might see a daily post from myself in your feed. Nothing too intrusive, I promise.

Follow me on Twitter

If you're more of a twitterer I tweet under the handle @dellagalton. The odd re-tweet would be most appreciated.

You can follow me here: twitter.com/dellagalton

Review this book

Positive reviews are always welcome. You don't have to have bought this book on amazon to leave your glowing five star endorsement.

Got a blog or a podcast?

A book review, or a link to my website (www.dellagalton.co.uk) are always appreciated. And if you'd like to interview me for your blog or podcast, just drop me a line.

Tell a friend
And finally, one of the hardest things for any author to achieve is 'word of mouth' recommendations. Next time you find yourself discussing books with a friend, remember me! :-)

Lots of love

Della

Also Available

The Short Story Writer's Toolshed
Your Quick Read, Straight-to-the-Point Guide
to Writing & Selling Short Fiction
by Della Galton

The Short Story Writer's Toolshed

Originally written as a series for Writers' Forum Magazine, this snappy, no-nonsense guide has been expanded, amended and updated. Using new examples from her own published short fiction, Della Galton takes you from 'story idea' to 'final edit', and demonstrates how to construct and polish the perfect short story, ready for publication.

Della Galton is a working writer and agony aunt for Writers' Forum. She has had three novels and over 1000 short stories published.

"Writing advice from one of the best in the business."
Carl Styants, Editor of Writers' Forum Magazine

VISIT AMAZON TO
BUY THE BOOK
AND FIND OUT MORE DELLA'S NON-FICTION AT
DELLAGALTON.CO.UK

Also Available

Ice And A Slice
The third full-length novel from
Della Galton

Ice And A Slice

Life should be idyllic, and it pretty much is for Sarah-Jane. Marriage to Tom is wonderful, even if he is hardly ever home. And lots of people have catastrophic fall-outs with their sister, don't they? They're bound to make it up some day. Just not right now, OK! And as for her drinking, yes it's true, she occasionally has one glass of wine too many, but everyone does that. It's hardly a massive problem, is it? Her best friend, Tanya, has much worse problems. Sarah-Jane's determined to help her out with them – just as soon as she's convinced Kit, the very nice man at the addiction clinic, that she's perfectly fine.

She is perfectly fine, isn't she?

Praise for Della's novels
"Della's writing is stylish, moving, original and fun : a wonderfully satisfying journey to a destination you can eagerly anticipate without ever guessing."
Liz Smith, Fiction Editor, My Weekly

Also Available

Ten Weeks To Target
One of several novellas by Della Galton.
Now available as an ebook, and in paperback

Ten Weeks To Target

Divorcee Janine has outgrown her entire wardrobe. Her niece's wedding is in ten weeks. Drastic action is needed. She joins a slimming club where she meets Pete, whose wife has given him an ultimatum: 'Lose four stone or I'm leaving you'… The two support each other through the dramas of life, as well as slimming, but reaching their targets turns out to be a new beginning – in more ways than one.

Available now from amazon
and wherever you purchased this book,
along with…

The Wish List
Genre: Romance / Comedy

Shadowman
Genre: Cosy Crime / Thriller

Meltwater
Genre: Romance / Family

Also Available

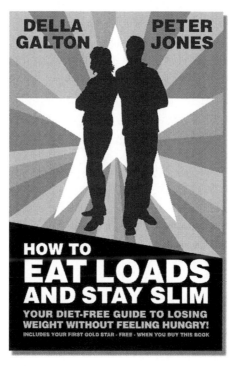

How To Eat Loads And Stay Slim
Your diet-free guide to losing weight
without feeling hungry!
By Della Galton & Peter Jones

How To Eat Loads And Stay Slim

How To Eat Loads and Stay Slim isn't a diet book. Not in the traditional sense.

It's a mixture of hard science (eg. how hunger really works), quick 'cheats' (eg. how to make zero fat chips), psychological techniques (eg. why focusing on your food as you eat is really important), ingenious strategies (eg. how to cut down on sugar without going cold turkey), and easy peasy recipes (eg. Peter's roast potato & egg smashup breakfast or Della's apple ginger clafouti) – all served up in an easy-to-digest, humourous read from authors who've been where you are now.

Each thought provoking, scientifically-provable, idea has a STAR RATING. There are fifty four stars available. You get one just for buying the book! Collect enough and you'll steadily increase your chances of being able to eat loads AND stay slim. Collect enough stars (thirty or more would be a good target to have) and we personally guarantee that a slim figure, coupled with a healthy but satiated appetite, are yours for the taking. No dieting required.

'HOW TO EAT LOADS AND STAY SLIM'
IS AVAILABLE IN PAPERBACK FROM ALL GOOD
BOOKSTORES, AS AN E-BOOK FOR ALL E-READING DEVICES,
AND AS AN AUDIO DOWNLOAD FROM AUDIBLE (.CO.UK & .COM).

FIND OUT MORE AT
WWW.HOWTOEATLOADSANDSTAYSLIM.COM

46157810R00063

Printed in Poland
by Amazon Fulfillment
Poland Sp. z o.o., Wrocław